TUAREGS

ANNA CAREY SABBAH

SMART APPLE MEDIA MANKATO MINNESOTA

Published by Smart Apple Media
123 South Broad Street, Mankato, Minnesota 56001

Copyright © 2000 Smart Apple Media.
Produced by The Creative Spark, San Juan Capistrano, CA
    Editor: Elizabeth Sirimarco
    Designer: Mary Francis-DeMarois
    Art Direction: Robert Court
    Page Layout: Jo Maurine Wheeler

Photos/Illustrations: Wofgang Kaehler/Corbis 4, 20; Kevin Davidson 6;
Tiziana and Gianni Baldizzone/Corbis 7, 19, 23, 24; Christine Osborne/
Corbis 8; Caroline Penn 9; Betty Press/Woodfin Camp/PNI 11, 29; Maggie
Steber/Aurora 12, 16, 19; Bernard and Catherine Desjeux/Corbis 14; Nik
Wheeler/Corbis 15; Stefano Amantini/Bruce Coleman/PNI 17; Juan
Echeverria/Corbis 26; Victor Englebright 27

Library of Congress Cataloging-in-Publication Data
Sabbah, Ann Carey, 1965–
    Tuareg / Ann Carey Sabbah.
        p. cm. — (Endangered cultures)
    Includes index.
    Summary: Details the history, life, traditions, and culture of the
Tuareg people of the deserts of northern Africa.
    ISBN 1-887068-93-7 (alk. paper)
    1. Tuaregs—Juvenile literature. [1. Tuaregs] I. Title. II. Series.
DT346.T7S22 1999
961'.004933—dc21   98-46705

First edition

9   8   7   6   5   4   3   2   1

Table of Contents

During the brief Saharan cold season, which lasts from December through March, high winds and sand storms are common.

A Desert People

In the vast, harsh lands of northern Africa live a group of people called the Tuareg. For centuries they have roamed the region's deserts and semideserts, moving across what is now southern Algeria and Libya and into northern Mali and Niger. At the heart of their homeland is the Sahara, the world's largest desert. It stretches across northern Africa for more than 3,000 miles (4,830 kilometers)—an area larger than the **contiguous** United States. Many Tuareg also live in the Sahel, a semidesert region south of the Sahara.

Estimates suggest that there are about one million Tuareg in the region today. Many are **nomads**, traveling in search of water for themselves and their livestock, as well as fertile land where they can grow crops. In the past, the most important members of their society traveled in great camel **caravans**, transporting precious goods across the desert.

Life in the Sahara Desert is difficult. High, rocky mountains shape the landscape, and the wind forms rolling dunes by molding waves of sand around large rocks. The climate of the Sahara is extreme and dry. Daytime temperatures in the brief cold season can still rise to 110°F (43°C) and higher, yet at night the temperatures can fall to nearly freezing. Daytime temperatures during the hot season can soar to 130°F (55°C).

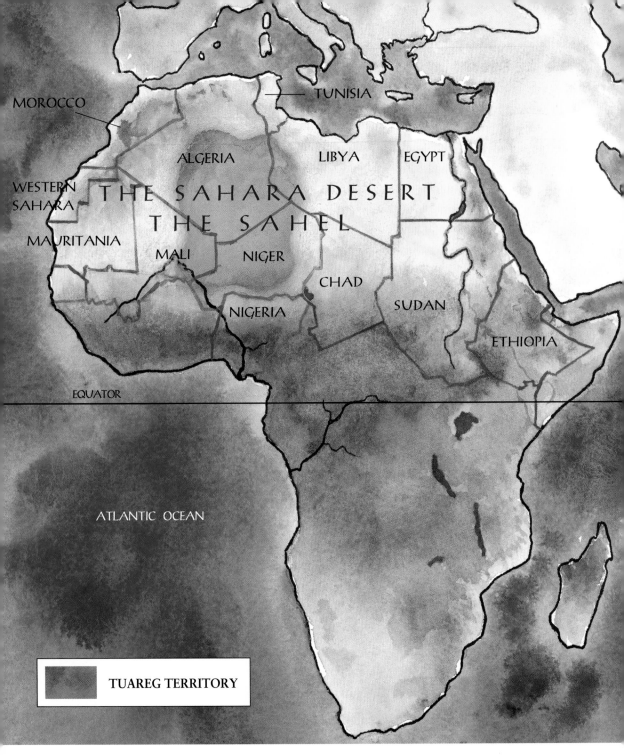

MOROCCO

TUNISIA

ALGERIA

LIBYA

EGYPT

WESTERN
SAHARA

THE SAHARA DESERT
THE SAHEL

MAURITANIA

MALI

NIGER

CHAD

NIGERIA

SUDAN

ETHIOPIA

EQUATOR

ATLANTIC OCEAN

TUAREG TERRITORY

*Toward the end of the 20th century, many Tuareg moved farther south into the Sahel—
a semidesert region south of the Sahara—to escape the drought and famine that have become
all too common in the Sahara. Most Tuareg live in the Sahara and the Sahel of Mali and Niger.*

On average, less than two inches (five centimeters) of rain fall each year in the Sahara. It is nearly impossible for most plants to grow. Only in the Sahel, where there is slightly more precipitation, can vegetation survive. Even in this more temperate climate, annual rainfall generally amounts only to between four and eight inches (10 to 20 centimeters).

3000 B.C.

The Berber ancestors of the Tuareg arrive on the Mediterranean coast of North Africa.

The extreme climate of the Sahara and the Sahel makes it nearly impossible to grow crops in most places. The Tuareg set up camps or villages near an oasis, providing them with the water they need to survive.

The Tuareg live in the extreme climate of North Africa, a region so remote that few other people come into contact with them.

The few plants that do grow in the Sahara must be hardy enough to withstand the deadly heat and nighttime chill. They have thick bark and waxy leaves that keep the plants from drying out. Desert plants have other traits adapted to the desert as well. The acacia tree is covered with thorns that prevent animals from eating its leaves. The date palm has tough, rubbery leaves and long roots that can reach far down into the soil to find water.

A Tuareg family and their livestock herds may travel as far as 1,000 miles (1,600 kilometers) in a single year. Travel is done on foot or on the back of a camel. The Tuareg roam until they find a suitable place with a good source of water and enough plant life to support them. An area in the desert where a steady source of water makes farming possible is called an oasis.

711

Arabs conquer North Africa. Waves of people, including those who would become the Tuareg, migrate to the south and settle in the desert.

THE CAMEL

Camels are well adapted to the harsh life in the Sahara. They have big feet that are flat on the bottom, preventing them from sinking into the soft sand. Their low, flat nostrils and long, thick eyelashes keep the sand out of their nose and eyes. Most important, the hump on their back stores water as fat so they can travel long distances across the dry desert without needing much water. They are sometimes called the Ship of the Desert because they provide such a reliable form of transportation. A camel can go for days without food and weeks without water. The Tuareg consider the camel so valuable that a young man often offers a camel to the father of the young woman he wants to marry.

The Berbers control much of North Africa.

The Tuareg attempt to leave their camp before the water dries up and the vegetation is gone. Moving on allows the grasses and plants a chance to grow back. If people and animals put too much stress on a fertile piece of land, the resources will not be available in the future. The Tuareg use their resources wisely and know how important it is to conserve them.

A Tuareg family with a large herd of animals is considered wealthy. Not only do the animals provide food and leather, they give a family something to trade for other goods. Camels are the most important animals of all. Without them, it would be nearly impossible to live as nomads. Unlike other camels, the **dromedaries** raised by the Tuareg have only one hump on their backs. Dromedaries are also called Arabian camels.

Camels can carry people and their possessions for long distances across the desert. Having the ability to store water in their humps allows camels to function for much longer without a water source than other animals. Tuareg families often travel at least 100 miles (160 kilometers) to find a place with enough water nearby to support them, and this takes days to accomplish.

Because nomadic Tuareg move so often, they live in tents that can be easily set up or taken down. They make their tents with pieces of cloth or leather draped over wooden posts. Thick straw mats, called *asabers*, line the walls, and these are held together with long strips of leather. *Asabers* keep out the day's heat, as well as blowing sand.

A **nuclear family** typically lives together in a tent or hut, and a village is often made up of an **extended family**. Sometimes many families band together to travel from place to place. A group also may form a more permanent village near a source of water in a more fertile area where they can grow crops. These less-nomadic Tuareg live in cone-shaped huts made from grass, and wealthier families may live in sturdier houses made of mud or stone.

1400s

The Tuareg establish the Sultanate of Aïr.

When Tuareg families settle in an area for longer periods, they may construct semi-permanent huts of grass and mud.

The Tuareg have been called the Blue People because they traditionally wore clothing made from indigo-dyed fabric.

The Blue People

The Tuareg have been called the Blue People and the People of the Veil because of their distinctive clothing. Tuareg men wear long, loose robes. This clothing shields them from the desert's blinding sun and blowing sand. They wrap their heads and faces with a long piece of cloth called a *tagelmust*. From about the age of 18, a Tuareg man always wears his *tagelmust* when he is with someone from outside his family. The more important his companions, the higher he will wear it on his face. With a chief or elder, for example, the *tagelmust* is worn high on the face, covering both the nose and mouth. A man may even eat and drink wearing his *tagelmust*, passing a spoon or cup underneath the cloth.

A Tuareg woman also wears long, loose cotton robes and turbans to shield her skin, but unlike the men, she does not cover her face. Instead, she wears a head scarf after marriage to communicate her status as a married woman.

The fabric used to make the Tuareg's garments is often dyed with indigo, a blue dye made from a variety of plants. With so little water available, the Tuareg cannot afford to waste it dying cloth, so they pound indigo powder into it with stones. When the cloth is worn close to the body,

The height of the Aïr Empire, in which the Tuareg control North African trade routes and conquer neighboring states.

the dye sometimes stains the skin blue, and thus the Tuareg have been called the Blue People. In the past, if a Tuareg man had particularly dark, blue skin, he was considered powerful and important.

The Tuareg live in a matriarchal society, which means the women are well respected and have a certain amount of power. Legend says the Tuareg descended from the daughters of a single woman, and the women have enjoyed economic independence and high social status ever since. In more recent times, the beliefs of **Islam**, the most common religion of the Tuareg, have made family ties based on the father more significant, but women continue to have power within their community.

DESERT MUSIC

Among the Tuareg, musicians are usually the women and girls. One instrument they play is called the *anzad*, a type of violin with one string. They also make drums from hollowed gourds and wooden bowls. The musicians beat the drums to call villagers together for a feast, called an *ahal*. At an *ahal*, the girls and women clap their hands and sing songs that tell stories. The men, carrying their spears and swords, ride camels in a circle around the women.

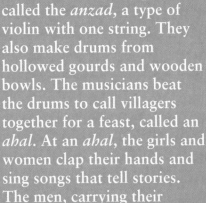

A bride's female relatives build a tent to offer as a **dowry** when she marries, and the woman will own the tent throughout her life. Tuareg women decide where a group will set up a village. A woman may also inherit a portion of her father's possessions, including his camels or his garden.

1899

French colonialists begin their fight to control the region in which the Tuareg live.

A tagelmust may be more than 20 feet (six meters) long when the fabric is stretched out. This traditional garment protects the head and face from the sun. It is also believed to protect the wearer from evil spirits that might enter through the nose and mouth.

The French conquer the Aïr Empire, which becomes part of the French West Africa colony.

The Tuareg believe they descended from a single woman and her daughters. This legend continues to influence modern Tuareg, who still honor and respect the women of their society.

Women care for their families, harvest family gardens, and make the *asabers* that cover the walls and floor of the tent. Tuareg women are skilled with their hands and craft a variety of beautiful objects, such as tents, sword sheaths, clothing ornaments, and bags used to carry water. They make leather from animal hides, rubbing them with clay or acacia bark to make them waterproof. Young girls learn all these skills by helping their mothers.

While women own animals and land, only the men plant and irrigate gardens or participate in trading caravans. Men also tend to the animals. Young boys are responsible for the animals, too. A 12-year-old boy might care for an entire herd of 10 or 15 animals all by himself or herd a group of camels by walking toward them and waving a long stick.

Tuareg men still use their camels to make long trips across the desert. Trade has always been important to the Tuareg, but today there are fewer goods for them to transport. The most important trade commodity is now salt. A Tuareg caravan might make a journey of 600 miles (960 kilometers) across the desert to carry salt from the mines. Once they reach their destination, the travelers trade the salt for things they need—just as in centuries past. Then they make the long journey back to their families. A caravan trip can take two months or even longer.

1917

The Tuareg rebel unsuccessfully against French colonialists.

A Tuareg caravan prepares to depart on its journey across the desert.

The French West Africa colony comes to an end, and North African nation-states are established.

At the end of a camel race, it is not important which contestant was the fastest, but who was the most skillful and fearless rider.

The Tuareg ride their camels not just for work or travel, but also for fun. Sometimes they race their camels. The men and the boys wear their best robes and *tagelmusts*. They use ashes to darken their eyebrows and the skin around their eyes and put their finest blankets, saddles, and stirrups on the camels. A large group will start by walking the camels across the sand. Suddenly someone will give a shout, and the race begins. The men are careful to display their best riding skills.

Even though the name Tuareg comes from the word *tarek* meaning "those who abandoned God," most Tuareg are Muslims, which means they practice the religion of Islam. Muslims believe the doctrines of Islam were handed down from their God, who they call Allah, through a series of human messengers. Their holy book, the **Koran**, contains the revelations given to Muhammad, the most important prophet of Islam.

A Tuareg holy man is called a *marabout*. He teaches the children how to read lessons from the *Koran* and officiates at important events, such as weddings and funerals. The Tuareg also believe the *marabout* has a special power to bless others, called *al baraka*.

The Tuareg speak a language called Tamacheq and write in an ancient Libyan script called Tifnagh. Unlike many other forms of written language, Tifnagh can be read left to right, right to left, or top to bottom. In some parts of the Sahara, Tuareg ancestors etched Tifnagh script into rocks to record important events in their history. One Tuareg legend says a mythical hero named Aligouran was the author of these ancient messages.

1967 – 1973

A devastating drought strikes Tuareg territory.

Tuareg artisans craft beautiful items from leather and metal.

19

Two Tuareg warriors perform a dance with swords during a feast.

The History of the Tuareg

The ancestors of the Tuareg were people called **Berbers**. They lived along the coast of northern Africa about five thousand years ago. When the Arab invaders conquered North Africa in the eighth century, the people migrated south and settled in the desert. These people eventually became known as the Tuareg.

Over the next few hundred years, the Tuareg expanded into other regions of the Sahara, gradually gaining control of the most important trade routes across northern Africa. The Tuareg camel caravans traveled one of the main trans-Saharan trade routes across the desert to the Mediterranean coast where ships waited to take goods to Europe. The shipping hub of Africa at the time was Tripoli, capital of the country now called Libya.

By the 14th century, the Tuareg were the most powerful people in the desert of northern Africa. They transported valuable goods back and forth across the Sahara in huge caravans that sometimes included thousands of camels. Tuareg caravans traveled great distances.

Among the rare goods the Tuareg transported were gold, ebony, ivory, spices, and ostrich feathers. They also transported valuable salt and dates along the trade routes.

Sometimes the Tuareg caravanners owned these goods, other times they transported them for other people. They traded these precious items for money or for things they could not easily obtain, such as metal tools, grain, weapons, cloth, and rugs. The Tuareg were also involved in the slave trade, transporting other Africans to the Mediterranean coast where they were crowded onto boats. These people were then sent to the United States and other countries and sold as slaves.

The Tuareg formed a powerful state in what is now central Niger. It was called the **Sultanate** of Aïr, and its capital was the city of Agadez. Aïr controlled the trade routes and grew more powerful by conquering the neighboring states during the 17th and 18th centuries. The Aïr Empire reached the height of its power in the 19th century.

By 1900, the French had invaded the Tuareg empire, and it became part of the French West Africa colony. The Tuareg wanted their independence and had no interest in joining a European colony, so they rebelled against French rule in 1917. Many died in the fierce battle that resulted, and about 30,000 Tuareg fled south to Nigeria.

By the 1960s, the French were no longer in power, and the Tuareg found their territory divided into new nations— Algeria, Libya, Mali, and Niger. They had first resisted the French, and now they opposed the governments of the new nations, refusing to pay taxes or send their children to state-run schools.

Each new nation had rules about who could cross the borders and when they could do so. The Tuareg were used to moving about freely without thinking about national boundaries, but borders quickly changed their traditional patterns of grazing and travel. Droughts made it more difficult to find suitable pasture and farming land. Salt, which had become the Tuareg's major commodity, decreased in value. Such changes threatened to destroy the traditional lifestyle of the Tuareg.

1990s

Tuareg rebellions occur in Niger and Mali.

The Tuareg first gained control of important North African trade routes in the 14th century.

23

The Tuareg have always valued the independence of their nomadic way of life, but now many have been forced to settle in the cities and towns of North Africa.

Change Among
The Tuareg

The world around the Tuareg is changing rapidly. Merchants no longer need them to carry goods. Today the majority of the people in the countries where the Tuareg live lead a settled lifestyle. The governments of Algeria, Libya, Mali, and Niger have decided that the Tuareg should settle as well and have tried to put an end to their traditional nomadic ways. The Algerian government went so far as to force groups of Tuareg to live on farming cooperatives.

Because the governments of Libya and Algeria have such strict laws about the number of camel caravans allowed to cross their borders each year, many Tuareg have chosen to move south to Mali and Niger. In addition, developers have built roads across the desert, so few people need camel caravans to transport goods these days. In recent years, the caravan trade only remains strong between Niger and Nigeria.

Adding to their difficulties, two severe droughts hit the region in the last decades of the 20th century. The first lasted five years, from 1967 to 1973. It destroyed pastures and much of the Tuareg's life-sustaining livestock, ultimately killing thousands of people.

TUAREG SOCIETY

The Tuareg once had a strict social structure. There were five main classes—the nobles (*imjeghen*), the noble's tenants (*imghad*), the artisans (*inaden*), the servants (*iklan*), and the serfs (*ighawalen*). Nobles usually controlled the caravan trade, owned most of the camels, and were more nomadic than other Tuareg. They traveled nearly seven months of the year and returned to a village or oasis only to collect their portion of the harvest. The *imghad* often rented land from the nobles to grow gardens or graze livestock. The *inaden* were skilled metal and leather workers, who made beautiful jewelry, tools, weapons, and decorative clothing. They also performed songs and told stories for noble families. Servants and serfs tended the noble's gardens and homes. Usually Tuareg married within their own social class. The changing world that surrounds the Tuareg have made these social classes less distinct than they once were, especially in villages. Most Tuareg must combine a variety of occupations to support their families. Camel caravans have become increasingly rare, and individuals from every social class tend their own gardens and herd whatever livestock they may have.

The Sahelian drought of 1984 and 1985 caused many Tuareg to migrate north from Mali and Niger into Algeria and Libya. A group of Tuareg men who called themselves *ishumar*, which means to be unemployed, received military training and weapons while living in Libya. When they tried to return to Mali and Niger, the governments of those countries, still trying to keep nomads from roaming within their borders, stopped them. The Tuareg, many armed with weapons from Libya, started a rebellion to preserve their way of life. This resulted in years of warfare in some parts of Mali and Niger. In 1994, a peace agreement was finally reached in Niger, but the rebellion lasted until 1995 in Mali.

1994

Tuareg rebels sign a peace agreement in Niger.

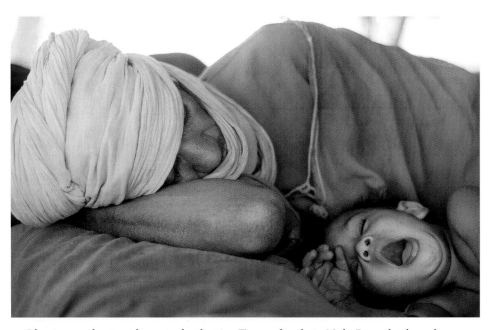

Blowing sand enters the tent of a sleeping Tuareg family in Mali. Droughts have forever changed the Tuareg's homeland, and lands that could once support crops and livestock are now desert.

27

Many survivors of the droughts decided to sell what remained of their herds and move into towns, looking for work as migrant farmers, metal workers, or guards. Much of the land where the Tuareg lived is now unusable for grazing and farming. **Desertification** threatens the Sahel and the northern parts of the Sahara. The climate continues to change all around the world, and the Tuareg believe the rainfall is less than it had been before the droughts. Scientists who investigate **global warming** suspect that the Tuareg's territory could get even drier as the Earth's climate continues to heat up.

As populations grow in the shrinking area of the Sahel, shepherds graze too many animals in too small an area of land. Farmers clear much of the land of all wild vegetation. They do not allow the time necessary for fields

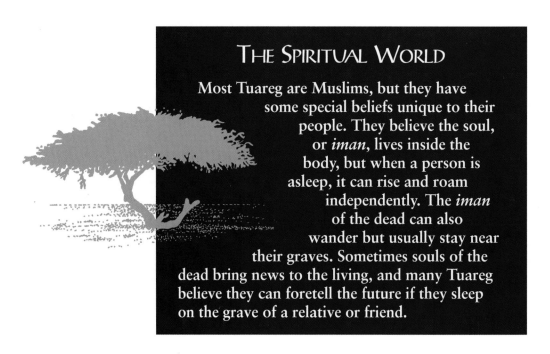

THE SPIRITUAL WORLD

Most Tuareg are Muslims, but they have some special beliefs unique to their people. They believe the soul, or *iman*, lives inside the body, but when a person is asleep, it can rise and roam independently. The *iman* of the dead can also wander but usually stay near their graves. Sometimes souls of the dead bring news to the living, and many Tuareg believe they can foretell the future if they sleep on the grave of a relative or friend.

to recover, so the soil becomes dry and fragile, causing further desertification and reducing the areas in which the Tuareg can set up camp.

As necessity forces the Tuareg to settle in one place, many aspects of their culture disappear. They build stationary homes of mud, stone, or sod instead of living in tents. They begin to rely more on cultivating crops than on herding animals. When drought and desertification make farming impossible, some take jobs with companies that drill for oil in the desert. Others work in the port cities of North and West Africa.

The Tuareg have an old expression: To wander is to be free, but to live a settled life is to be shackled. As the Tuareg lose their free and nomadic life, they also lose many of the traditions that make their culture unique. Moving into the 21st century, the future of North Africa's nomads grows increasingly uncertain.

1998

Tuareg in Mali and Niger try to resume their nomadic lifestyle but meet resistance from the governments of the two countries.

Political tensions and natural disasters have forever changed the Tuareg way of life.

Glossary

Berbers   A group of Caucasian, or non-black, people of Northern Africa.

caravans   Groups of people traveling together, often utilizing pack animals.

contiguous   To be attached or connected. The contiguous United States are those that are attached to one another geographically, which excludes Alaska and Hawaii.

cooperatives   Farms where people work together to produce food.

desertification   The process by which grazing or farming land becomes a desert because of climate changes or overuse of the land.

dowry   Money or goods that a woman's family gives her and her new husband when they marry.

dromedaries   Camels with a single hump. Camels with two humps are called Bactrian camels.

extended family   A family that includes, in addition to the nuclear family of parents and their children, uncles and aunts, their children, and the grandparents of the family.

global warming   An increase in the average temperature of the earth's climate. Some scientists believe global warming is caused by the burning of fossil fuels.

Islam	The religion of the Muslim people. About one-fifth of the world population practices Islam.
Koran	The religious text of Islam, including revelations made to Muhammad by Allah from 610 to 632 B.C.
nomad	An individual who travels from place to place and does not have a fixed home.
nuclear family	A family group made of two parents and their children.
sultanate	A state or country governed by a sultan, a Muslim king.

Further Reading and Information

BOOKS:
Bailey, Donna. *Nomads*. Austin, TX: Steck-Vaughn, 1990.
Jenkins, Martin. *Deserts*. Minneapolis, MN: The Lerner Publishing Group, 1996.
Raskin, Lawrence. *52 Days by Camel: My Sahara Adventure*. Toronto, Canada: Annick Press, 1998.
Reynolds, Jan. *Sahara*. San Diego, CA: Harcourt-Brace, 1991.

WEB SITES:
http://www.csmonitor.com/durable/1997/09/09/intl/intl.4.html
http://www.outside.starwave.com/magazine/1097/9710forbid.html

Index

Items in bold print indicate illustration.